Grades 6-10

PEARSON LANGUAGE CENTRAL

ELD

PEARSON

Upper Saddle River, New Jersey • Shoreview, Minnesota
Glenview, Illinois • Boston, Massachusetts • Chandler, Arizona

ISBN-13: 978-0-13-367580-1
ISBN-10:   0-13-367580-7

4 5 6 7 8 9 10   V011 14 13 12 11 10

Table of Contents

Welcome to School!

Today is your first day at school.

Students come on a **bus**.

They cross the street at the **crosswalk**.

They go in through the **door**.

Students go to the **office** for information.

Students put books and coats in a **locker**.

Then they go to their **home room**.

Students go up
the stairs to class.

Students go down
the stairs to class.

A student
uses a ramp.

Students walk
in the hall.

Students read and study in the **library**.

Students play sports in **gym** class.

Students sing in the **music room**.

Students draw and paint in **art class**.

They drink from
the **water fountain**.

When students get
hurt, they go to the
nurse's office.

It is time for lunch. Students
eat in the **cafeteria**.

Students ask to use
the **rest room**.

Students come to the
auditorium for an assembly.

Students use the **computer
lab** to write reports.

School is over. Students get books from their lockers.

1 At School

Tell what you know.

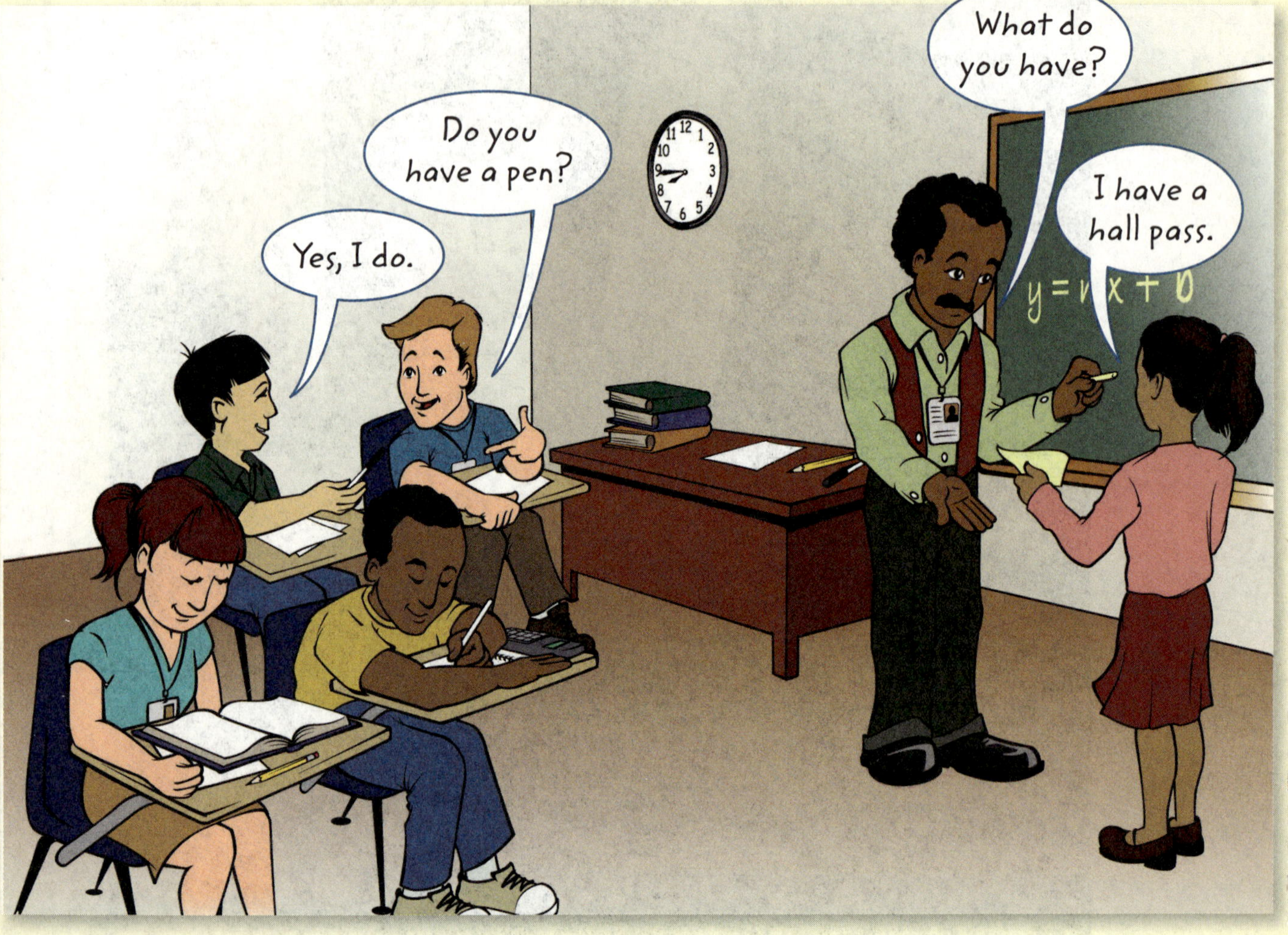

Look at the pictures. Say the words.

Say more words.

What do you have?

I have a calculator.

I have an eraser.

I have the book.

Answer the questions.

Check the column to show if you have or don't have these things.

Do you have ______ ?	Yes, I do.	No, I don't.
a book	☐	☐
a notebook	☐	☐
a pencil	☐	☐
a pen	☐	☐
an eraser	☐	☐
an ID	☐	☐
a calculator	☐	☐

Label the school items.

1. 

2. 

3. 

4. 

____

5. 

6. 

7. 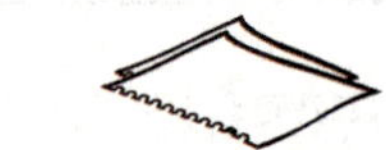

8. 

____

9. 

10. 

____

Ask a partner.

1. Do you have a pen and a pencil? Yes, I do./No, I don't.

2. Do you have a calculator? Yes, I __________ ./No, I __________ .

3. Do you have the book? Yes, __________ ./No, __________ .

4. What do you have? I have __________ .

Complete these sentences using the pictures.

1. I have ________________________ and ________________________. 

2. I don't have ________________________. 

3. I have ________________________ and ________________________.

4. I have ________________________ and ________________________. 

Circle the word that names the picture.

1. 

notebook   eraser

2. 

pencil   pen

3. 

ID   calculator

4. 

desk   book

I can.

☐ I can name things at school.

☐ I can write about things I have in school.

☐ I can talk to friends about what I have.

Tell what you know.

Look at the pictures. Say the words.

letter   address

area code

phone number

Say more words.

Where do I live?

I live on Main Street.

I live at 233 Elm Street.

I live in a house in Los Angeles, California.

Write your information.

Complete the information about yourself.

My name is ________________________ . I live in a/an ________________________ .
                                                                                (house/apartment)

My street address is ____ .
                                 (number, street name)

________________ , ________ , ________
(city)   (state)   (zip code)

My phone number is (______) ______ – ______ .
(area code)

Write the words.

1. 

2. 

3. 

4. 

Ask a partner.

1. What city do you live in? I live in the city of _________ .

2. What state do you live in? I live in the state of _________ .

3. What is your street address? My street address is _________ .

4. What is the area code for your phone number? My area code is _________ .

5. What is your phone number? My phone number is _________ .

Complete these sentences about yourself.

1. Where do you live? I _____________________ in a(n) _____________________ .

2. I use the phone to call people. First, I need an _____________________ and a

   _____________________ .

3. I can send a _____________________ to a friend. First, I need an

   _____________________ .

4. Someday I want to live in my own _____________________ or

   _____________________ .

5. My street address is _____________________ .

Draw a line to connect the question with the answer.

Say them with a partner.

What is your zip code?	(213) 555-7846
What city do you live in?	My zip code is 90027.
What's your address?	47 Elm Street, Los Angeles, California.
What's your phone number?	Yes, I do live in an apartment.
Do you live in an apartment?	I live in Los Angeles.

I can.

☐ I can ask people where they live.

☐ I can tell my address and phone number.

☐ I can talk with others about where they live.

3 At Home

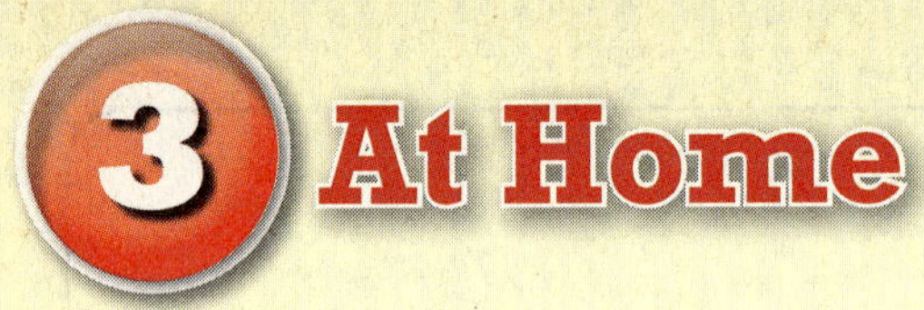

Tell what you know.

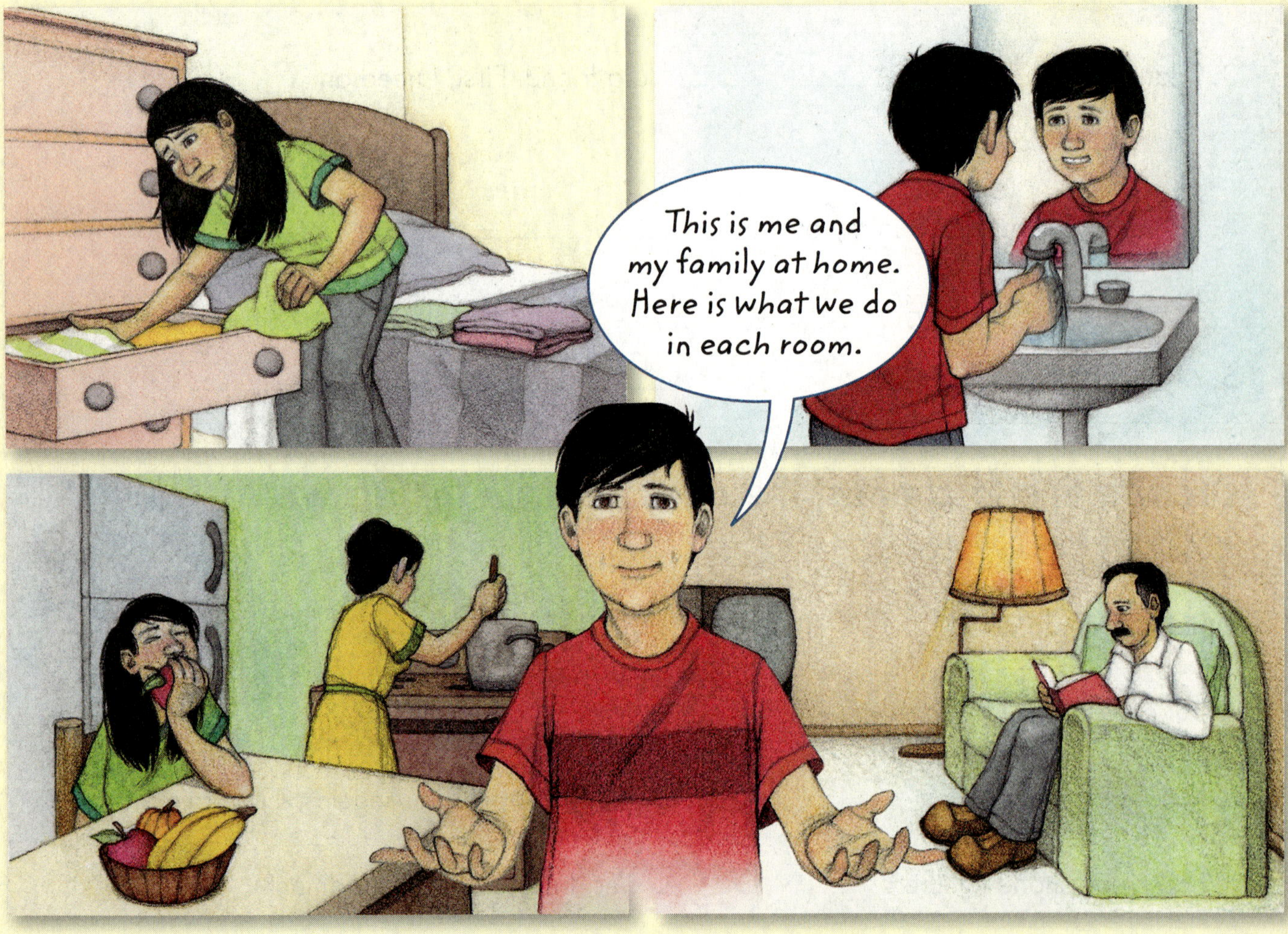

Look at the pictures. Say the words.

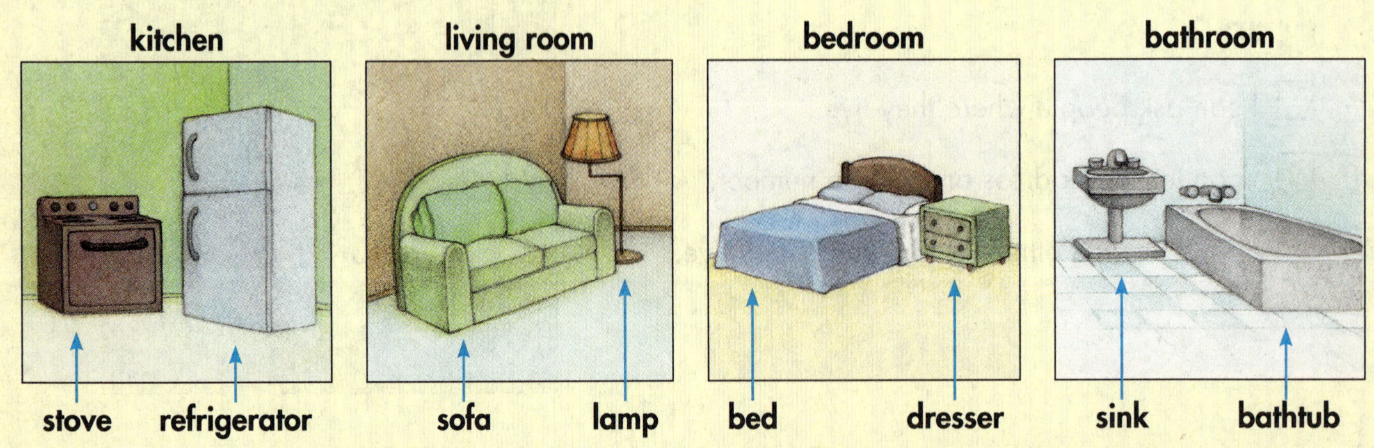

Say more words.

make food, eat

read, watch TV

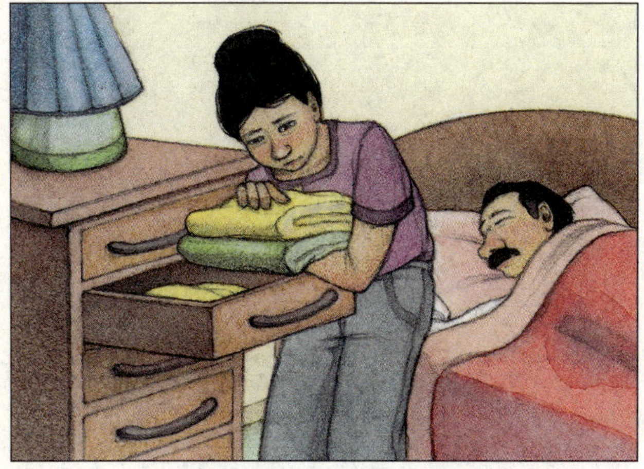

put away clothes, sleep

wash hands

Answer the questions.

Where do you _____ ?	in the bedroom	in the bathroom	in the kitchen	in the living room
eat	☐	☐	☑	☑
watch TV	☐	☐	☐	☐
read	☐	☐	☐	☐
put away clothes	☐	☐	☐	☐
wash your hands	☐	☐	☐	☐
make food	☐	☐	☐	☐
sleep	☐	☐	☐	☐

Label the rooms. Then label the things.

1. _______________

2. _______________

3. _______________

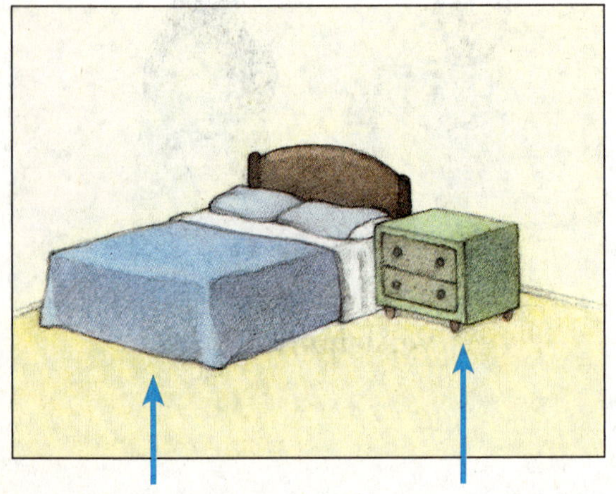

4. _______________

Ask a partner.

1. What's in your bedroom? There is a _________ and a _________ in my bedroom.

2. What's in your living room? There is a _________ and a _________ in my living room.

3. What's in your kitchen? There is a _________ and a _________ in my kitchen.

4. What's in your bathroom? There is a _________ and a _________ in my bathroom.

Complete these sentences about yourself.

1. I ________________________ and ________________________ in the kitchen.

2. I ________________________ and ________________________ in the living room.

3. I sleep in the ________________________ .

4. I wash my hands in the ________________________ .

5. Where do you do your homework? I do my homework in the ________________________ .

6. Where do you read? I read in the ________________________ .

Circle the word that does not fit.

1. bedroom   living room   bathroom   sink

2. eat   bedroom   wash hands   watch TV

3. sleep   bed   dresser   lamp

4. make food   read   stove   put away clothes

5. refrigerator   kitchen   bathtub   sink

I can.

☐ I can name the rooms in a home.

☐ I can name and write about things in a home.

☐ I can talk to friends about what I do at home.

4 My Family

Tell what you know.

Look at the pictures. Say the words.

grandmother

sister

brother

grandfather

aunt

mother

father

uncle

Say more words.

I feel happy.

My brother and I feel sad.

My father is angry.

They are scared.

Answer the questions.

How do you feel when you___?	happy	sad	angry	scared
are with your family	☐	☐	☐	☐
finish school	☐	☐	☐	☐
do not know anybody	☐	☐	☐	☐
are alone	☐	☐	☐	☐
can't watch TV	☐	☐	☐	☐
have free time	☐	☐	☐	☐

Who are these people? Write the words.

1.  

2.  

3.  

4.  

Ask a partner.

1. Who is the oldest person in your family? The oldest person in my family is __________ .

2. What is your mother's name? My mother's name is __________ .

3. What is your father's name? My father's name is __________ .

4. How many brothers do you have? I have __________ brothers./I don't have any brothers.

5. How many sisters do you have? I have __________ sisters./I don't have any sisters.

Complete these sentences about yourself.

1. At home, I live with _________________ .

2. A person in my family who makes me feel happy is _________________ .

3. A person in my family who makes me feel angry is _________________ .

4. How do you feel when you go to school? I feel _________________ .

5. How do you feel when you leave school? I feel _________________ .

Circle the word that does not fit.

1.	brother	sister	father	scared
2.	father	mother	grandmother	angry
3.	sad	angry	father	happy
4.	happy	smile	aunt	laugh
5.	uncle	aunt	mother	school

I can.

☐ I can name the people in my family.

☐ I can write about the people in a family.

☐ I can talk to friends about how I feel.

Tell what you know.

Student Schedule	Monday	Tuesday	Wednesday	Thursday	Friday
Math	8:15	8:15	8:15	8:15	8:15
Science	9:15	9:15	9:15	9:15	9:15
English	10:30	10:30	10:30	10:30	10:30
Social Studies	1:00	1:00	1:00	1:00	1:00
Computer Lab			2:00		
Physical Education	2:00				2:00
Art		2:00		2:00	

schedule

Look at the pictures. Say the words.

math

science

physical education

English

social studies

art

Say more words.

Today is Monday.
Luis has social studies class at one o'clock.

It's a quarter after two on Wednesday.
Where is Luis?

Luis and Samira have art class on Tuesdays and Thursdays.
Art is their favorite class. What time is it?

Complete the schedule.

	Monday	Tuesday	_______	Thursday	_______
_______	1:00	1:00	1:00	1:00	1:00
_______			2:00		
_______		2:00		2:00	

What time is it?

Write the words.

1. It's twelve ________________________ .

2. It's a ________________________ to five.

3. 9:15 = a ________________________ after nine

4. 6:30 = ________________________ ________________________

5. 11:45 = a ________________________ to twelve

When do you have class?

Class	Day(s)	Time
1.		
2.		
3.		

Ask a partner.

1. When do you have math class? I have math class on ________ .

2. What class do you have on Friday? I have ________ on Friday.

3. What time is English class? English class is at ________ .

4. What time is it? It's ________ .

5. What is your favorite class? My favorite class is ________ .

Match the question with the answer.

Draw a line.

What's today?   I have art class on Wednesdays.

Do you have math class today?   It's quarter to ten.

What is your favorite class?   It's Wednesday.

When do you have art class?   Yes, I do.

What time is it?   My favorite class is social studies.

Write about yourself.

1. I have math class on ________________ .

2. I have English class on ________________ .

3. I have ________________ on Mondays at ________________ .

4. Today is ________________ . My next class is ________________ .

5. My favorite class is ________________ . It's at ________________ .

6. My favorite day of the school week is ________________ .

I can.

☐ I can name school subjects, days of the week, months, and times.

☐ I can write about school subjects and schedules.

☐ I can talk to friends about when I do things at school.

Tell what you know.

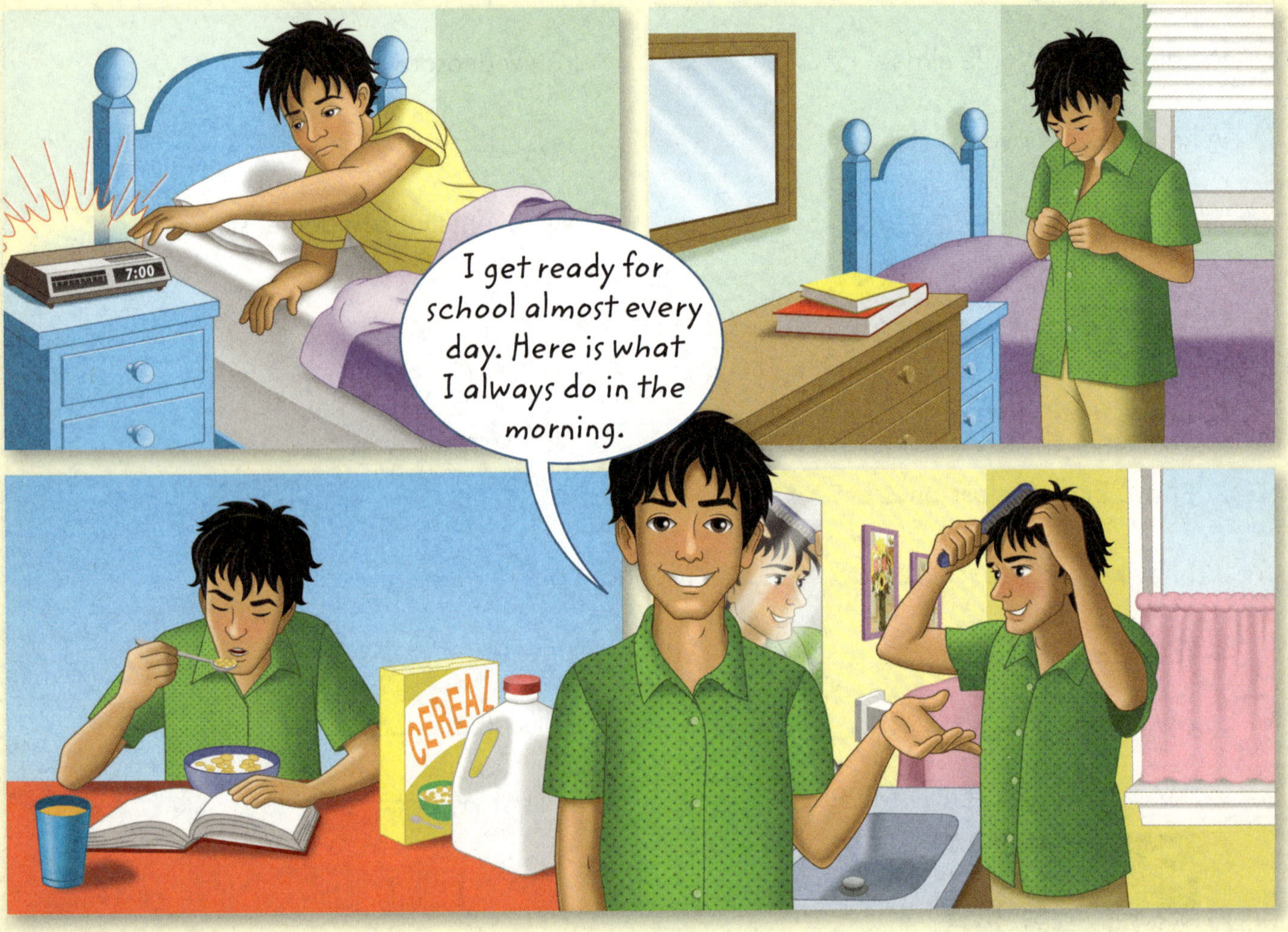

Look at the pictures. Say the words.

wake up

get dressed

have breakfast

brush teeth

brush hair

Say more words.

always    never

always	Monday	Tuesday	Wednesday	Thursday	Friday	Saturday	Sunday
often		Tuesday	Wednesday		Friday		Sunday
sometimes	Monday			Thursday			
never							

Answer the questions.

How often do you ______ ?	always	often	sometimes	never
take a shower	☐	☐	☐	☐
brush your teeth	☐	☐	☐	☐
brush your hair	☐	☐	☐	☐
put on clean clothes	☐	☐	☐	☐
have breakfast	☐	☐	☐	☐
study	☐	☐	☐	☐
ride the bus	☐	☐	☐	☐

Write the name of the activity.

1. 

2. 

3. 

4. 

5. 

Ask a partner.

1. How often do you have breakfast? I __________ have breakfast.

2. How often do you brush your teeth? I __________ brush my teeth.

3. How often do you take the bus? I __________ take the bus.

4. How often do you study? I __________ study.

Complete these sentences about yourself.

| take a shower | get up | eat | ride | brush my teeth | study |

1. I _________________________ every day.

2. I sometimes _________________________ breakfast.

3. I always _________________________ in the morning.

4. I often _________________________ after school.

5. I _________________________ the bus to school.

Circle the word that does not belong.

1. always   often   get up   never

2. wake up   drink   toothbrush   eat

3. sometimes   study   brush hair   talk

I can.

☐ I can name things people do to get ready for school.

☐ I can talk and write about how often I do things.

☐ I can talk to friends about what I do to get ready for school.

7

Getting Ready

Tell what you know.

Look at the pictures. Say the words.

How is the weather?

It's raining.

It's sunny.

It's snowing.

It's cloudy.

It's windy.

Answer the questions.

What do you wear when it's _____ ?	snowing	sunny	raining
jacket	✔	☐	☐
raincoat	☐	☐	☐
T-shirt	☐	☐	☐
shorts	☐	☐	☐
sweater	☐	☐	☐
pants	☐	☐	☐
sneakers	☐	☐	☐

Write the words.

1. _______________

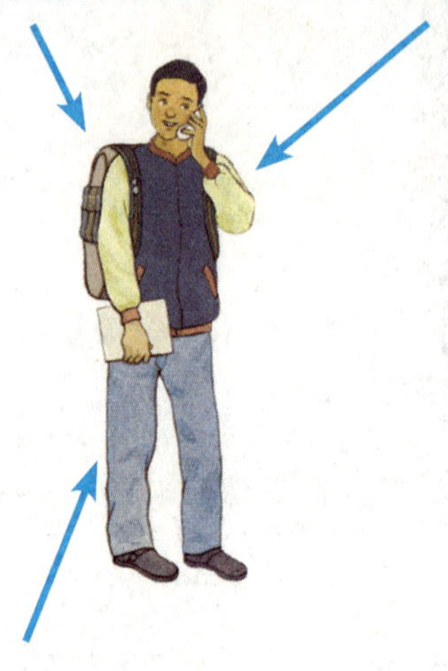

____

2. _______________

____

3. _______________

____

4. _______________

____

Ask a partner.

1. What are you wearing? I'm wearing _________ .

2. What do you have? I have _________ .

3. What do you wear when it is sunny? I wear a _________ .

4. What do you wear when it is raining? I wear a _________ and have an _________ .

Complete these sentences about yourself.

1. When it's raining, I wear a ___________________ .

2. Now I am wearing ___________________ .

3. When it's sunny, I wear a ___________________ .

4. I have an umbrella when it's ___________________ .

5. When it's snowing, I can't wear a ___________________ .

6. I have a ___________________ to carry books.

Circle the word that does not fit.

1. cloudy   windy   shorts

2. umbrella   raincoat   T-shirt

3. pants   wearing   jeans

4. raincoat   jacket   shoes

5. sneakers   shoes   backpack

6. raining   snowing   skirt

I can.

☐ I can name the things that I wear.

☐ I can write about the weather.

☐ I can talk to friends about what they wear.

Tell what you know.

Look at the pictures. Say the words.

using a computer

using a calculator

studying   reading

listening   writing

taking notes

drawing

What are they doing?

They are sitting. He is raising his hand.

They are standing and waiting in line.

They are running. He is walking.

They are working in science class.

Answer the questions.

Check the class or classes where you are doing these things.

I am _____ .	in math class	in science class	in gym class	in art class
studying	☐	☐	☐	☐
reading	☐	☐	☐	☐
listening	☐	☐	☐	☐
drawing	☐	☐	☐	☐
taking notes	☐	☐	☐	☐
using a computer	☐	☐	☐	☐

What are they doing? Complete the sentences.

1. **They are** _______________ .

2. **She is** _______________ .

They are _______________ .

3. **He is** _______________ .

4. **She is** _______________ .

Ask a partner.

1. What is he doing in math class? He's ________ .

2. What is she doing in art class? She's ________ .

3. What are they doing in the library? They're ________ .

4. What are we doing in gym class? We're ________ .

5. What are you doing in science class? I'm ________ .

Complete these sentences about yourself.

Tell what you are doing.

1. I'm ________________________ in math class.

2. I'm ________________________ in art class.

3. I'm ________________________ in gym class.

4. I'm sitting ________________________ .

5. Right now, I'm ________________________ .

6. Who is standing? ________________________ is standing.

Use the words. Tell what the person is doing.

1. She, use, computer   *She is using a computer* .

2. I, read ________________________ .

3. They, study ________________________ .

4. We, listen ________________________ .

5. He, takes notes ________________________ .

6. You, raise, hand ________________________ .

I can.

☐ I can tell what I am doing at school.

☐ I can talk and write about working at school.

☐ I can talk to friends about what I do at school.

My Week at School

Tell what you know.

month day year

APRIL 2008

Sunday	Monday	Tuesday	Wednesday	Thursday	Friday	Saturday
			1	2	3	4	5
6	7	8	9	10	11	12
13	14	15	16	17	18	19
20	21	22	23	24	25	26
27	28	29	30			

two days ago today last week

date

Wednesday, April 16, 2008

journal

Look at the pictures. Say the words.

yesterday

day year

2 days ago

last night

today

Say more words.

I fixed a chair in school. I used a hammer.

Yesterday, I was at home.
Today, I planted flowers at school.

I painted in art class.
I studied for a test at home.

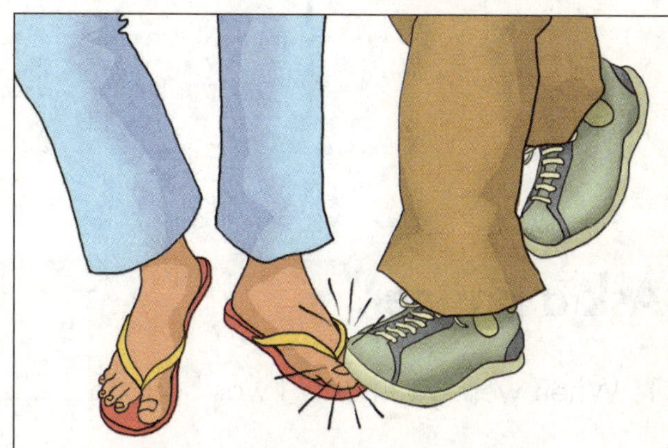

Today, I danced in gym class.

How long ago did you do these things?

When was the last time you ______ ?	a week ago or longer	yesterday	last night	today
danced	☐	☐	☐	✔
painted	☐	☐	☐	☐
fixed something	☐	☐	☐	☐
studied	☐	☐	☐	☐
used a hammer	☐	☐	☐	☐
worked	☐	☐	☐	☐

Write the parts of the calendar and the journal.

1.

2.

______ ______ ______

Ask a partner.

1. When were you born? I was born on ________ .

2. What was the date two days ago? It was ________ two days ago.

3. What was the date yesterday? Yesterday was ________ .

4. What did you do last night? I ________ last night.

5. What did you do today? Today, I ________ .

Complete these sentences.

1. What day of the week is it today? Today is ________________________ .

2. What month is it? ________________________

3. What year is it? ________________________

4. What can you write in to tell what happened today? I can write in a ________________________ .

5. What is something you did in school a month ago? A month ago, I ________________________ .

Think about things that happened.

Circle the word that does not belong.

1. played   used   dance   studied

2. painted   planting   fixed   played

3. use   studied   planted   walked

4. play   used   fixed   painted

5. planted   fix   danced   was

I can.

☐ I can name the date in a journal and on a calendar.

☐ I can name the things that happen in time order.

☐ I can talk to friends about what I did at school.

Read the story. Tell what you know.

Yesterday, I **felt** sick.

First, I **told** my teacher.

Then, I **went** to the nurse's office.

Next, I **drank** some water and **ate** some crackers.

Finally, I **went** home and **went** to bed.

Today, I **feel** better.

Talk about Jaleel's day in the present and past tenses.

Jaleel **felt** sick yesterday.

He **feels** better.

He **told** his teacher he was sick.

He **tells** his teacher thank you.

Yesterday, he **went** to the nurse's office.

He **goes** to art class today.

He **drank** water yesterday.

Today, he **drinks** chocolate milk.

Yesterday, he **ate** crackers.

He **eats** pizza for lunch today.

Put the story in order.

Write the numbers 1–4 in the boxes below.

- [ ] **Then**, he drank water and ate some crackers.
- [ ] **First**, Jaleel told his teacher.
- [ ] **Next**, he went to the nurse's office.
- [ ] **Finally**, he went home and went to bed.

Complete this chart.

present tense	past tense
eat	
	drank
feel	
go	
	told

Put these present tense sentences into the past tense.

1. She eats pizza for lunch. ____________________________ .

2. They go to the bus stop. ____________________________ .

3. He goes to art class. ____________________________ .

4. Jaleel drinks juice. ____________________________ .

5. Today, I feel happy. ____________________________ .

6. He tells his father about his day. ____________________________ .

Ask a partner.

1. How did you feel yesterday? I felt __________ .

2. Where did you go yesterday? I went __________ .

3. What did you eat yesterday? I ate __________ .

4. What did you drink yesterday? I drank __________ .

5. What did you tell your teacher yesterday? I told my teacher that __________ .

Complete the story.

Yesterday was a good day. I ________________ to school in the morning.

At lunchtime, I ________________ hungry so I ________________

to the cafeteria. I ________________ a salad and ________________

milk for lunch. I ________________ my friend about

my spelling test. I ________________ happy about

getting a good score.

Circle the word that does not fit.

1. first   finally   told   next
2. ate   drink   go   feel
3. yesterday   last night   nurse   today
4. then   eat   drink   tell
5. happy   sick   better   went

I can.

☐ I can tell the nurse that I am sick or have a stomachache.

☐ I can use *feel, eat, go, drink,* and *tell* correctly in the present and past tenses.

☐ I can use *first, next, then,* and *finally* correctly.

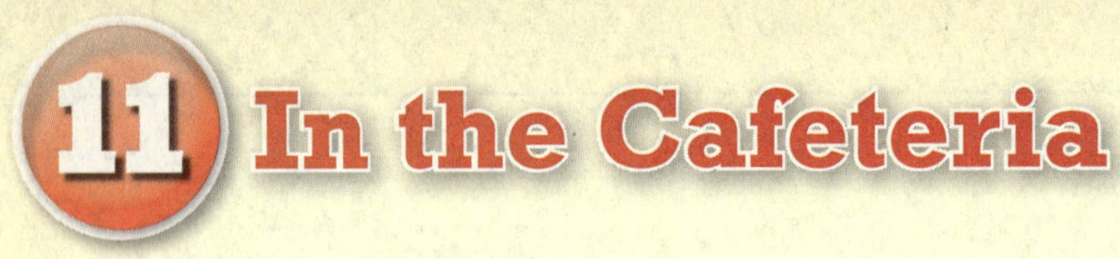

11 In the Cafeteria

Tell what you know.

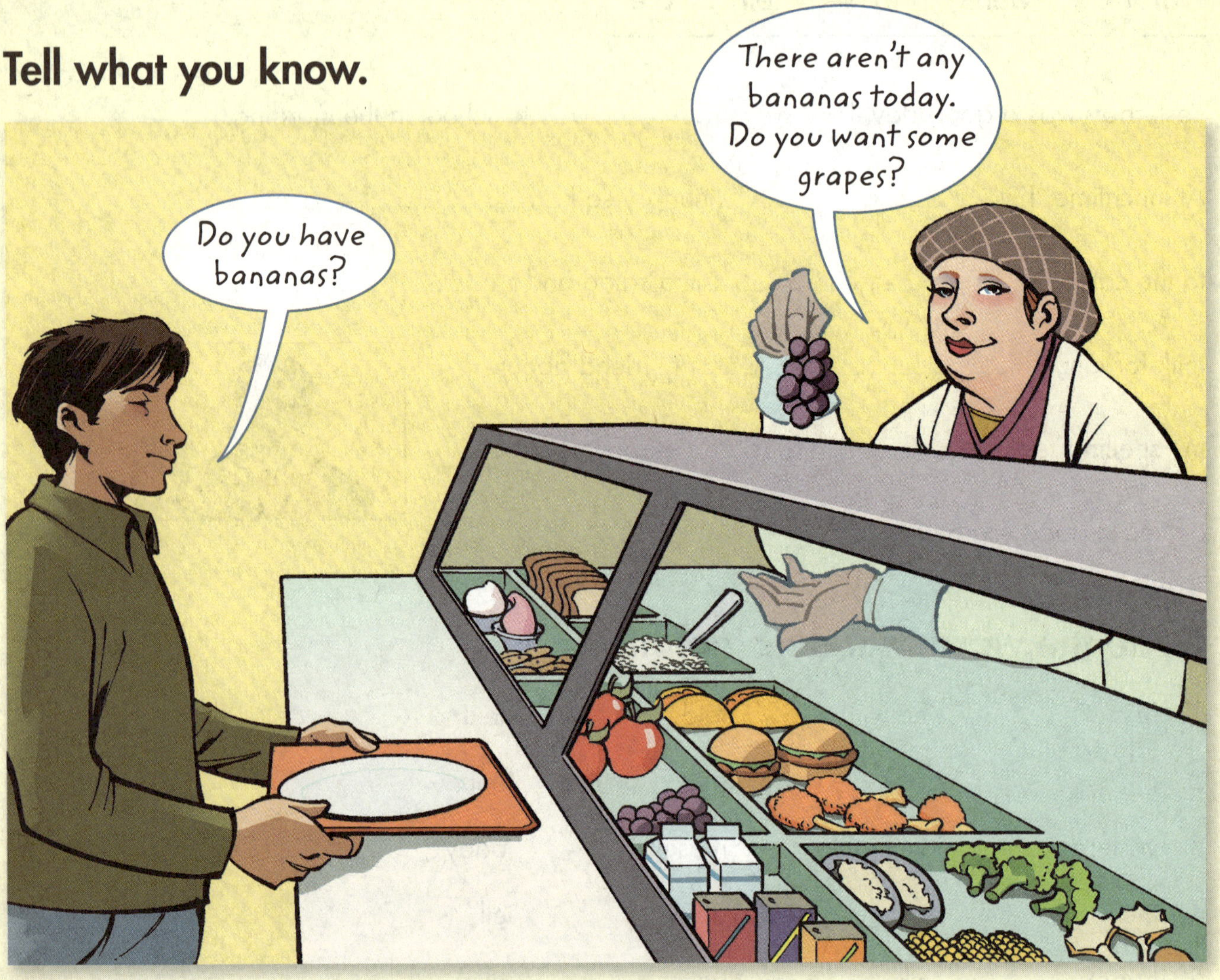

Do you have bananas?
There aren't any bananas today. Do you want some grapes?

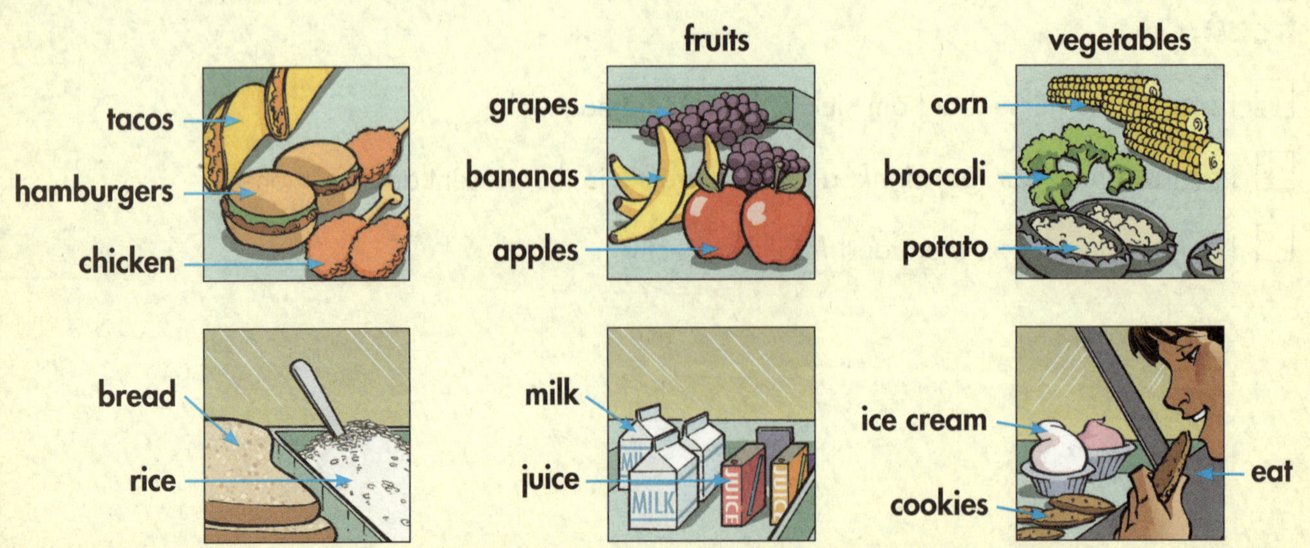

Look at the pictures. Say the words.

tacos
hamburgers
chicken

fruits
grapes
bananas
apples

vegetables
corn
broccoli
potato

bread
rice

milk
juice
MILK
JUICE

ice cream
cookies
eat

Say more words.

Look at the picture to the right. Then answer the questions.

Is there ______ ?	yes	no
a cookie	☐	☐
an apple	☐	☐
any broccoli	☐	☐
any chicken	☐	☐
any bread	☐	☐
a potato	☐	☐
any fruit	☐	☐
a taco	☐	☐
a hamburger	☐	☐
any corn	☐	☐

Write the words.

1. 

2. 

3. 

4. 

5. 

6. 

Ask a partner.

1. What vegetables do you like to eat? I like to eat __________ .

2. What is your favorite fruit to eat? My favorite fruit to eat is __________ .

3. What kind of food do you eat at home? I eat __________ at home.

4. What will you eat today? I will eat __________ today.

5. Is there any food that you do not eat? I never eat __________ .

Complete these sentences about yourself.

1. At school, I always eat ____________________ .

2. At home, I always eat ____________________ .

3. A vegetable I like to eat is ____________________ .

4. A fruit I sometimes eat is ____________________ .

5. A food I never eat is ____________________ .

6. After school, I like to eat a few ____________________ .

Circle the word that does not fit.

1. apple	banana	grapes	cookie
2. hamburger	taco	corn	chicken
3. juice	broccoli	potato	corn
4. few	some	any	eat
5. rice	bread	corn	some

I can.

☐ I can name and ask for food.

☐ I can talk and write about food.

☐ I can talk to friends about food.

12 After School

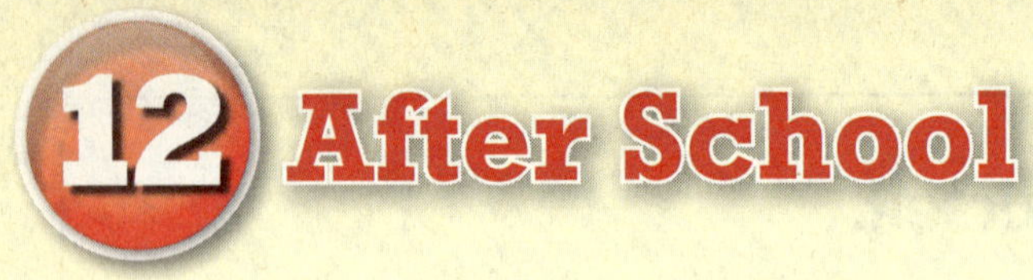

Tell what you know.

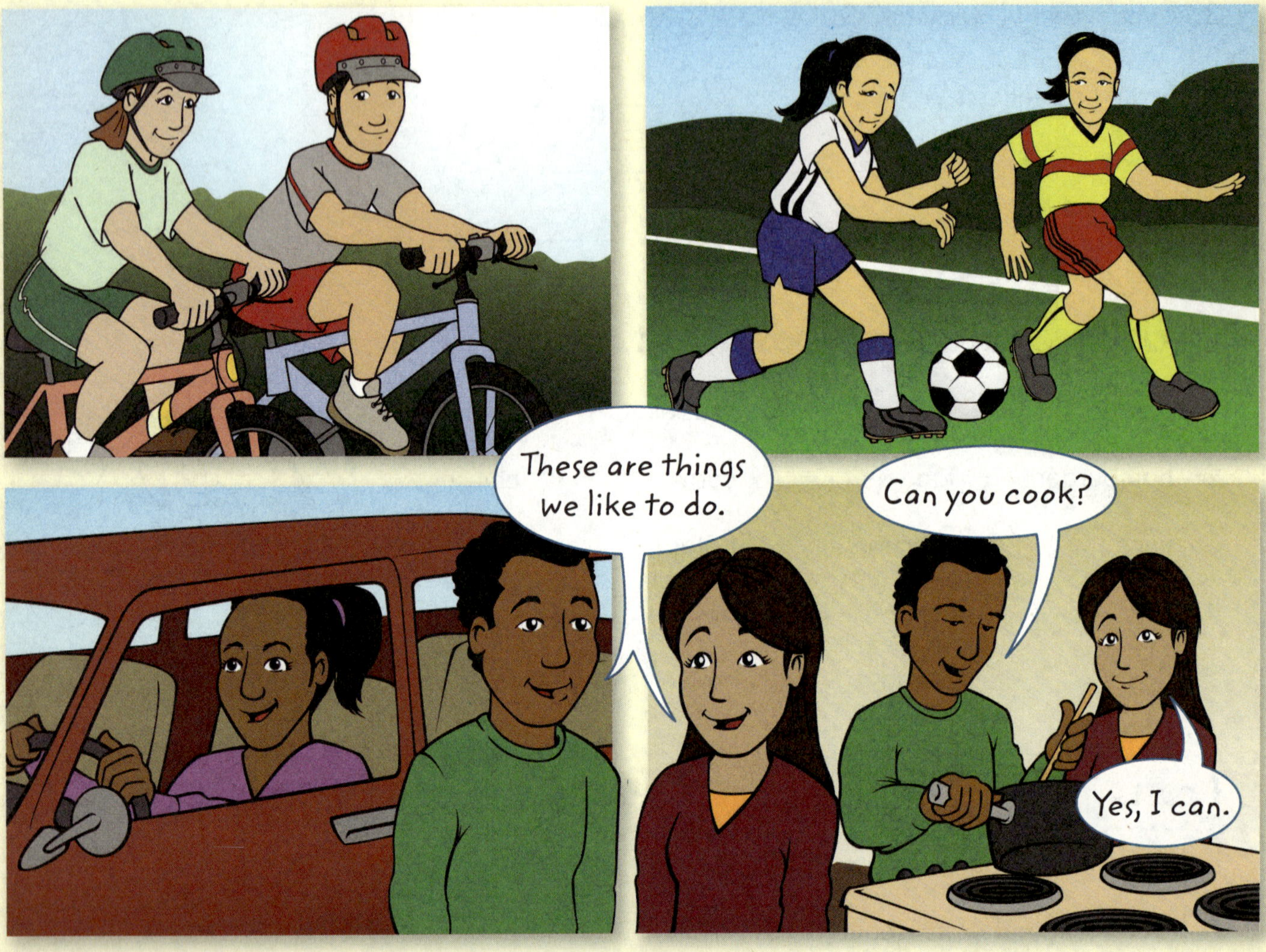

Look at the pictures. Say the words.

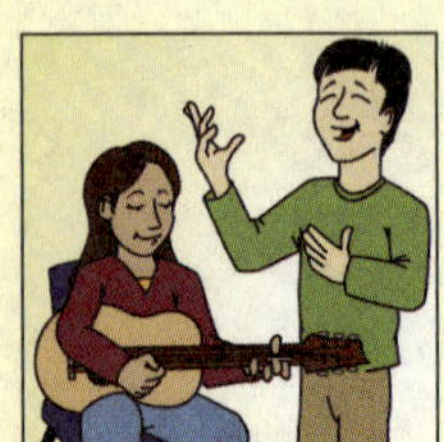

play the guitar
sing a song

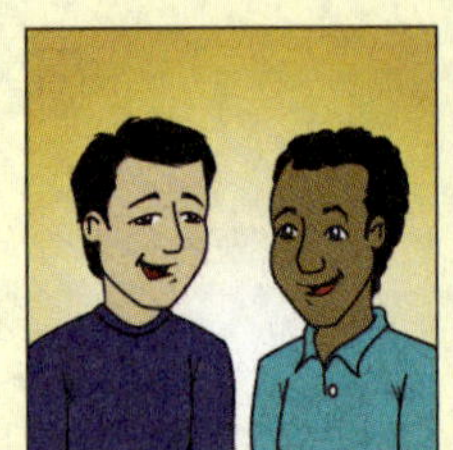

speak Japanese

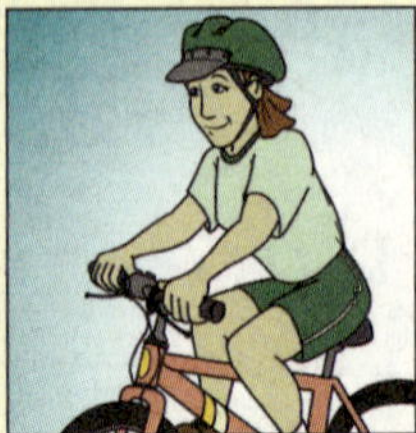

ride a bike

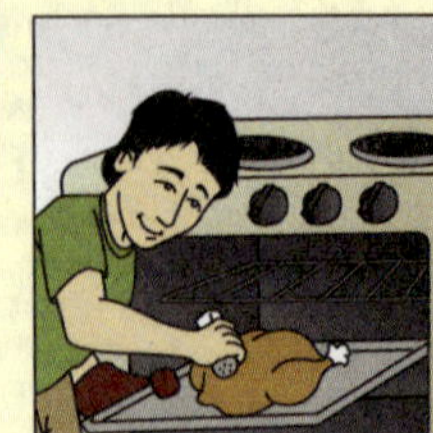

cook dinner

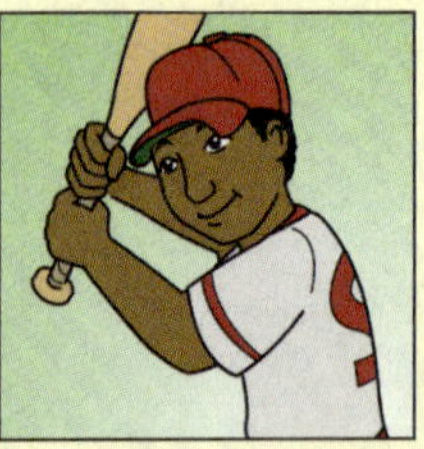

play baseball

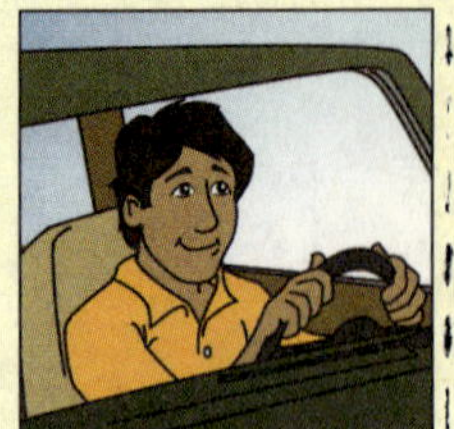

drive a car

Say more words.

Brandon likes to play the piano,
but he doesn't like to sing.

Amanda can't speak Spanish very well,
but she likes to practice.

Answer the questions.

Do you like to _____ ?	Yes, I do.	No, I don't.
sleep	☐	☐
watch TV	☐	☐
read	☐	☐
dance	☐	☐
study	☐	☐
clean	☐	☐
talk	☐	☐

Can you _____ ?	Yes, I can.	No, I can't.
speak Spanish	☐	☐
ride a bike	☐	☐
play the piano	☐	☐
play soccer	☐	☐
drive a car	☐	☐
sing a song	☐	☐
cook dinner	☐	☐

Write the action.

1. 

_________ the guitar

_________ a song

2. 

_________ a bike

3. 

_________ Japanese

4. 

_________ baseball

5. 

_________ dinner

6. 

_________ a car

Ask a partner.

1. Do you like to cook dinner? Yes, I do/No, I don't like to ________ .

2. What do you like to do after school? I like ________ .

3. Can you drive? Yes, ________ . /No, ________ .

4. What can you do very well? I can ________ .

5. What languages can you speak? I ________ .

Complete these sentences about yourself.

1. I like _________________________ on the weekends.

2. I don't like _________________________ after school.

3. I can _________________________ very well.

4. I can't _________________________ very well.

5. I can't play _________________________ .

6. I can play _________________________ .

Complete the conversation.

can	can't	like

Roberto: _________________ you speak Spanish?

Mary: No, I _________________ , but I would _________________ to learn.

Roberto: I _________________ help you learn a few words.

Mary: Great! I _________________ to practice speaking Spanish.

Roberto: ¡Perfecto! I _________________ speak Spanish and English.

I can.

☐ I can tell what I like to do.

☐ I can name things to do after school.

☐ I can talk to friends about what I like.

Tell what you know.

checking out a book

library

mailing a letter

post office

buying food

grocery store

waiting for a bus

bus stop

washing clothes

Laundromat

watching a movie

movie theater

Say more words.

to the right of

to the left

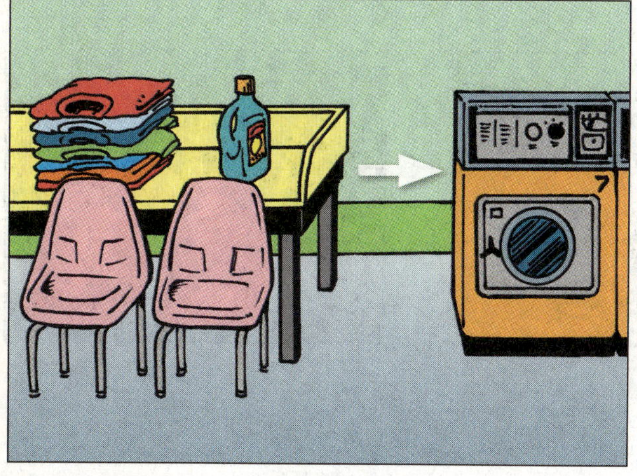

next to

across from

Answer the questions.

Check where you would go to do these things.

Where are you going to _____ ?	mail a letter	watch a movie	check out a book	buy food	wait for a bus	wash clothes
library	☐	☐	✓	☐	☐	☐
post office	☐	☐	☐	☐	☐	☐
grocery store	☐	☐	☐	☐	☐	☐
bus stop	☐	☐	☐	☐	☐	☐
Laundromat	☐	☐	☐	☐	☐	☐
movie theater	☐	☐	☐	☐	☐	☐

Where is it? What are they doing?

1. _______________

____

2. _______________

____

3. _______________

____

4. _______________

____

5. _______________

____

6. _______________

____

Ask a partner.

1. What are you doing at the movie theater? I am _________ .

2. What are you doing at the bus stop? I am _________ .

3. Who sits next to you in math class? _________ sits next to me.

4. Who sits to the right of you in science class? _________ sits to the right of me.

5. Who sits across from you in the cafeteria? _________ sits across from me.

Complete these sentences about yourself.

1. I am _________________________ at the grocery store.

2. I go to the _________________________ to mail letters.

3. I watch movies with friends at the _________________________ .

4. I stood _________________________ my friend at the bus stop.

5. I help my mother wash _________________________ at the _________________________ .

6. I go to the _________________________ to _________________________ books.

Circle the word that does not fit.

1. across from   to the right of   library

2. movie theater   Laundromat   watching a movie

3. next to   buying food   grocery store

4. post office   bus stop   mailing a letter

5. Laundromat   library   washing clothes

I can.

☐ I can name the places in a neighborhood.

☐ I can write about places in a neighborhood.

☐ I can talk to friends about what I do in my neighborhood.

Tell what you know.

Look at the pictures. Say the words.

mall

expensive

cheap

dollars and cents

need   old

cost   new

want   buy

five
dollars

ten
dollars

twenty
dollars

Say more words.

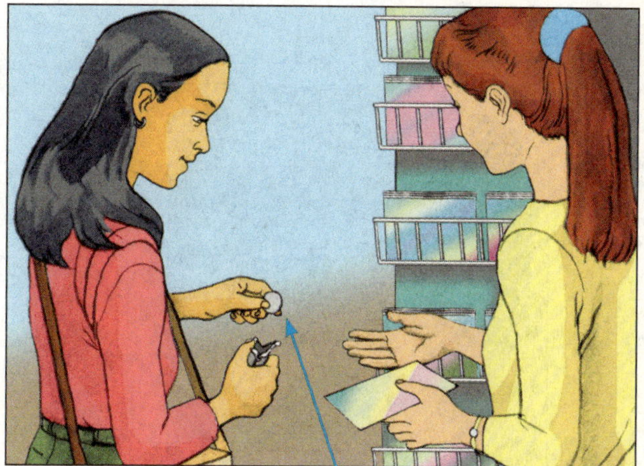

nickel   dime   change

quarter

more   less

penny

Answer the questions.

Check how much you think you could buy at the mall with the money amounts in the first column.

How much does it cost to ______?	buy a new CD	buy cheap earrings	play an old video game	buy an expensive T-shirt	go to a movie and buy popcorn
quarter	☐	☐	✔	☐	☐
five dollars	☐	☐	☐	☐	☐
ten dollars	☐	☐	☐	☐	☐
fifteen dollars	☐	☐	☐	☐	☐
twenty dollars	☐	☐	☐	☐	☐

Write the words.

1. ______________

______________   ______________

2. ______________

______________   ______________

3. ______________

______________   ______________

4. ______________

______________   ______________

Ask a partner.

1. What is one thing that you want to buy? I want to buy __________ .

2. What is one thing that you need to buy? I need to buy __________ .

3. Are clothes something you want or something you need? I __________ clothes.

4. Is going to a movie a want or a need? I __________ to go to a movie.

5. How much money do you take to the mall? I take __________ to the mall.

Fill in the blanks.

1. When I go to the mall, I like to _______________ .

2. I go to the mall when I need to buy _______________ .

3. If I want to buy _______________ I go to _______________ .

4. The most expensive thing I have ever bought is _______________ .

5. If I had ten dollars, I would buy _______________ .

6. If I had twenty dollars, I would buy _______________ .

Circle the word that does not belong.

1. five dollars	ten dollars	cookie	quarter
2. buy	need	penny	want
3. nickel	penny	dime	ten dollars
4. cost	buy	movie	need
5. jeans	shoes	jacket	expensive

I can.

☐ I can name things people do at the mall.

☐ I can talk about shopping and money.

☐ I can talk to friends about what I do at the mall.

Word Log

Write the words you learned.

p _ _ _

p _ _ _ _ _

e _ _ _ _ _

c _ _ _ _ _ _ _

n _ _ _ _ _ _ _

p _ _ _ _

d _ _ _ _

b _ _ _ _

l _ _

h _ _ _ _   p _ _ _

a or an?

_____ book

_____ ID

_____ calculator

_____ desk

_____ eraser

Do you have... ?

Circle the answer to each question about yourself.

1. Do you have a notebook?   Yes, I do.   No, I don't.
2. Do you have a book on your desk?   Yes, I do.   No, I don't.
3. Do you have paper in the notebook?   Yes, I do.   No, I don't.
4. Do you have an eraser on your pencil? Yes, I do.   No, I don't.
5. Do you have a pencil and a pen?   Yes, I do.   No, I don't.
6. Do you have an ID?   Yes, I do.   No, I don't.
7. Do you have a desk?   Yes, I do.   No, I don't.
8. Do you have a pencil on your desk?   Yes, I do.   No, I don't.
9. Do you have a hall pass?   Yes, I do.   No, I don't.
10. Do you have a calculator?   Yes, I do.   No, I don't.

What do you have?

Write 2–3 sentences about things at your school.

Write the words you learned.

Address Words

c _ _ _ _

z _ _ _ _   c _ _ _ _

s _ _ _ _   e

s _ _ _ _ _   t

Phone Words

p _ _ _ _ _   n _ _ _ _ _ _

a _ _ _ _   c _ _ _ _

Places to Live Words

h _ _ _ _ _

a _ _ _ _ _ _ _ _

Question Words

w _ _ _ e?

w _ _ t?

Action Words

l _ _ _ _

s _ _ _ _

Mail Words

a _ _ _ _ _ _ _ _

l _ _ _ _ _

Do you do this?

Circle the answer to each question.

1. Do you sleep in a stove? Yes, I do. (No, I don't.)
2. Do you eat in a living room? Yes, I do. No, I don't.
3. Do you wash your hands in a dresser? Yes, I do. No, I don't.
4. Do you make food in a bathtub? Yes, I do. No, I don't.
5. Do you watch TV in a bedroom? Yes, I do. No, I don't.
6. Do you stand on a lamp? Yes, I do. No, I don't.
7. Do you sleep on a sofa? Yes, I do. No, I don't.
8. Do you read on a chair? Yes, I do. No, I don't.
9. Do you wash clothes in a sink? Yes, I do. No, I don't.
10. Do you eat in a refrigerator? Yes, I do. No, I don't.

Write about your home.

What do you do at home? Where do you do it? What's in your bedroom?
Write 2–3 sentences about your home.

Word Log

Write the words you learned.

Family Words

m _ _ _ _ _

f _ _ _ _ _

b _ _ _ _ _

s _ _ _ _ _

u _ _ _ _

a _ _ _

g _ _ _ _ f _ _ _ _ _

g _ _ _ _ m _ _ _ _ _

Words that Tell About Me

h _ _ _ _

s _ _

a _ _ _ _

s _ _ _ _

f _ _ _

How do you feel?

Circle the answer to each question about yourself.

1. Do you smile when you are sad?   Yes, I do.   (No, I don't.)
2. Do you put away clothes when you are scared?   Yes, I do.   No, I don't.
3. Do you watch TV when you are angry?   Yes, I do.   No, I don't.
4. Do you sleep when you are happy?   Yes, I do.   No, I don't.
5. Do you cry when you are happy?   Yes, I do.   No, I don't.

Who is this person?

6. My father's brother is my __________ .   aunt   uncle   brother
7. My mother's father is my __________ .   uncle   brother   grandfather
8. My father's mother is my __________ .   aunt   grandmother   sister
9. My mother's sister is my __________ .   aunt   sister   grandmother
10. My father's mother is my __________ .   grandmother   aunt   sister

Write about your family.

Who are the people in your family? Write 2–3 sentences about them.

5 My School Schedule

Word Log

Write the words you learned.

School Subject Words

m _ _ _ _

s _ _ _ _ _ _ _

E _ _ _ _ _ _ _

s _ _ _ _ _ _   s _ _ _ _ _ _ _

c _ _ _ _ _ _ _ _ _   l _ _

a _ _ _

p _ _ _ _ _ _ _ _   e _ _ _ _ _ _ _ _ _

Day of the School Week Words

M _ _ _ _ _

T _ _ _ _ _ _

W _ _ _ _ _ _ _ _

T _ _ _ _ _ _ _

F _ _ _ _ _

Time Words

o' _ _ _ _ _ _

q _ _ _ _ _ _   a _ _ _ _ _

q _ _ _ _ _ _   t _ _

t _ _ _ _ _ _

True or False?

Answer the question about yourself.
If it is false, cross out the wrong word and write in a new one.

Example: _____*false*_____ I have art on ~~Mondays.~~ Wednesdays.

1. _____________ I have art every day.

2. _____________ It's twelve o'clock.

3. _____________ I have computer lab today.

4. _____________ Today is Friday.

5. _____________ My favorite class is math.

6. _____________ I go to school on Saturdays and Sundays.

7. _____________ I have English on Tuesdays.

8. _____________ My favorite day is Monday.

Write about your school schedule.

What is your schedule today? Write 2–3 sentences about your school schedule.

Every Day

Write the words you learned.

Every Day Words

w _ _ _   u _

g _ _   d _ _ _ _ _

h _ _ _   b _ _ _ _ _ _

b _ _ _ _ _ _   h _ _ _

When Words

e _ _ _ _ _   d _ _ _

a _ _ _ _ _ _ _

o _ _ _ _ _

s _ _ _ _ _ _ _ _

n _ _ _ _

Get to School Words

t _ _ _ _   b _ _ _

w _ _ _

Complete this paragraph about you.

Every morning, I wake up at ________________________ . The first thing that I do is

________________________ . Then, I go to the kitchen to ________________________ .

For breakfast, I always eat ________________________ and drink

________________________ . Next, I brush my ________________________ before I brush

my ________________________ . Finally, I go to school. I ________________________

to get to school. At school, I always ________________________ and

________________________ with my friends.

Write about getting ready for school.

What do you do to get ready for school? How often do you study or talk to friends?
How do you get to school? Write 2–3 sentences about getting ready for school.

____

____

____

____

____

Write the words you learned.

Weather Words

c _ _ _ _ _ _

s _ _ _ _ _ g

s _ _ _ _ _

r _ _ _ _ _

w _ _ _ _

Action Words

w _ _ _ _ _ _

Clothing Words

p _ _ _ _ _

i _ _ _ _

s _ _ _ _

Clothing and Things

When it's raining

r _ _ _ _ _ _ _

u _ _ _ _ _ _ _

When it's sunny

s _ _ _ _ _ _

T– _ _ _ _ _

When it's snowing

i _ _ _ _

s _ _ _ _ _ _

Wear on Your Feet

sh _ _ _

s _ _ _ _ _ _

Bring to School

b _ _ _ _ _ _

Do you do this?

Circle the answer to each question about yourself.

1. Do you wear shorts when it's snowing?   Yes, I do.   (No, I don't.)

2. Do you open an umbrella if it's sunny?   Yes, I do.   No, I don't.

3. Do you wear a jacket to put away clothes?   Yes, I do.   No, I don't.

4. Do you carry a backpack to school?   Yes, I do.   No, I don't.

5. Do you wear a backpack when you make a meal?   Yes, I do.   No, I don't.

6. Do you wear a raincoat to watch TV?   Yes, I do.   No, I don't.

7. Do you wear a jacket when it's snowing?   Yes, I do.   No, I don't.

8. Do you wear shoes when you sleep?   Yes, I do.   No, I don't.

9. Do you wear a T-shirt when it is raining?   Yes, I do.   No, I don't.

10. Do you bring an umbrella if it is windy?   Yes, I do.   No, I don't.

Write about what you are wearing.

What is the weather now? What did you wear to school today? Write 2–3 sentences.

Word Log

Write the words you learned.

In classes

u _ _ _ _ _ a computer

l _ _ _ _ _ _ _ g

r _ _ _ _ _ _

w _ _ _ _ _ _

w _ _ _ _ _

t _ _ _ _ _ notes

s _ _ _ _ _ _ _ in a chair

s _ _ _ _ _ _ _ for a test

s _ _ _ _ _ _ _ _ in line

r _ _ _ _ _ _ hands

d _ _ _ _ _ _ _ a picture

In gym

w _ _ _ _ _ _

r _ _ _ _ _ _

What are you doing?

Circle the answer to each question about yourself.

1. What are you doing in gym?   (running)   walking   sitting
2. What are you doing in math?   reading   adding   drawing
3. What are you doing in lunch?   eating   studying   sitting
4. What are you doing in art?   drawing   reading   standing
5. What are you doing in computer lab?   walking   writing   using a computer
6. What are you doing in social studies?   walking   raising hands   reading
7. What are you doing in science?   listening   studying   using a computer
8. What are you doing in home room?   taking notes   reading   standing
9. What are you doing in the afternoon?   working   drawing   subtracting
10. What are you doing in the morning?   walking   standing   working

Write about what you do at school.

What do you do at school? Write 2–3 sentences about your school work.

Word Log

Write the words you learned.

Calendar and Journal Words

d _ _ e

d _ _ _

m _ n _ _ _

ye _ _ _

w _ _ _ _

Past Action Words

u _ _ d

d _ _ c _ d

fi _ _ _ _

pl _ _ t _ _

s _ _ u _ i _ d

p _ i _ _ e _

Tuesday, April 15, 2008

Time Order Words

a week or two a _ _ _

l _ s _ _ n _ gh _ _

t _ d _ _

Did you do this?

Circle the answer to each question about yourself.

1. Did you plant flowers this month?   Yes, I did.   No, I did not.

2. Did you watch TV this morning?   Yes, I did.   No, I did not.

3. Did you fix something yesterday?   Yes, I did.   No, I did not.

4. Did you make a meal this week?   Yes, I did.   No, I did not.

5. Did you go to school last night?   Yes, I did.   No, I did not.

6. Did you study for a test last night?   Yes, I did.   No, I did not.

7. Did you have your birthday this month?   Yes, I did.   No, I did not.

8. Did you eat lunch today?   Yes, I did.   No, I did not.

9. Did you wear a jacket yesterday?   Yes, I did.   No, I did not.

10. Did you write in a journal?   Yes, I did.   No, I did not.

Write about what you did at school.

What did you do at school today? What did you do yesterday and last night?
Write 2–3 sentences about what you did.

Word Log

Write the words you learned.

Words About Being Sick

n _ _ _ _ _

s _ _ _ _ _ _ _ a _ _ _ _

s _ _ _ _

Present Tense Words

f _ _ _

g _

e _ _

d _ _ _ _

t _ _ _

Time Order Words

f _ _ _ _

n _ _ _

t _ _ _

f _ _ _ _ _ _ _

Past Tense Words

f _ _ _ _

w _ _ _ _

a _ _

d _ _ _ _

t _ _ _

Write about your lunch yesterday.

What did you eat for lunch yesterday? Where did you go? What did you eat and drink?
Write 4 sentences about your lunch. Draw pictures in the boxes.

1. First, _________________________ . 2. Next, _________________________ .

3. Then, _________________________ . 4. Finally, _________________________ .

Word Log

Write the words you learned.

Vegetables

p _ _ _ _ _ _

c _ _ _ _

b _ _ _ _ _ _ _

Action Word

e _ _

Words when I ask

m _ _

s _ _ _

t _ _ _ _

f _ _

a _ _

Drinks

j _ _ _ _

m _ _ _

Fruits

a _ _ _ _

b _ _ _ _ _

g _ _ _ _

Sweet Foods

c _ _ _ _ _ _

i _ _   c _ _ _ _

Meat

h _ _ _ _ _ _ _ _

c _ _ _ _ _

t _ _ _ _

Food Questions

Circle the answer to each question.

1. Can you drink a cookie?	Yes, I can.	(No, I can't.)
2. Is broccoli a vegetable?	Yes, it is.	No, it isn't.
3. Can you eat a potato?	Yes, I can.	No, I can't.
4. Is an apple a fruit?	Yes, it is.	No, it isn't.
5. Is corn a fruit?	Yes, it is.	No, it isn't.
6. Can you eat apple juice?	Yes, I can.	No, I can't.
7. Can you drink bread?	Yes, I can.	No, I can't.
8. Are grapes vegetables?	Yes, they are.	No, they aren't.
9. Do you like hamburgers?	Yes, I do.	No, I don't.
10. Can you eat rice?	Yes, I can.	No, I can't.

Write about what you eat.

What do you like to eat for lunch? What do you drink with your lunch?
Write two or three sentences about your favorite lunch.

____

____

____

____

Write the words you learned.

Action Words

p _ _ _ _   the guitar

s _ _ _ _   a song

s _ _ _ _ _   a language

p _ _ _ _   baseball

c _ _ _ _   dinner

d _ _ _ _ _   a car

r _ _ _ _   a bike

Ability Words

Yes, I c _ _ _ _ .

No, I c _ _ _ ' _ .

Like Words

I l _ _ _ _   to sing.

I d _ _ _ ' _   like to dance

Instrument Words

p _ _ _ _ _

g _ _ _ _ _ _

Sports Words

b _ _ _ _ _ _ _ _

s _ _ _ _ _

Play *I Can* Bingo.

Find someone you know who can do each of these things.

say *hello* in Spanish **Who?** _________	make breakfast **Who?** _________	sing a song **Who?** _________
drive a car **Who?** _________	play the drums **Who?** _________	dance very well **Who?** _________
whistle **Who?** _________	say "The Pledge of Allegiance" **Who?** _________	pat their head while rubbing their stomach **Who?** _________

Write about what you do.

What can you do the best? What do you like to do the most? Write two to three sentences.

____

____

____

____

Word Log

Write the words you learned.

Places Words

l _ _ _ _ _ _ _

b _ _ s _ _ _

m _ _ _ _ t _ _ _ _ _ _

g _ _ _ _ _ _ s _ _ _ _

p _ _ _ o _ _ _ _ _

L _ _ _ d _ _ _ t

Placement Words

t _ _ t _ _ _ r _ _ _ _ _ _ o _ the building

n _ _ _ _ t _ my brother

a _ _ _ _ _ _ f _ _ _ the librarian

t _ t _ _ _ l _ _ _ _ o _ the street sign

Doing things in the neighborhood

w _ _ t _ _ g f _ _ a b _ s

m _ _ l _ _ _ a l _ t _ _ _ _

w _ _ _ _ _ _ g a m _ v _ _ _

b _ y _ _ _ f _ o _ _ _

ch _ _ _ _ _ _ _ o _ _ a b _ _ _ _

wa _ _ _ _ _ _ cl _ _ _ _ _

Where do you go?

Circle the answer to each question about yourself.

1. Do you go to the post office to buy food?   Yes, I do.   (No, I don't.)
2. Do you go to the grocery store to check out a book?   Yes, I do.   No, I don't.
3. Do you go to a Laundromat to wash pants?   Yes, I do.   No, I don't.
4. Do you go to the bus stop to watch a movie?   Yes, I do.   No, I don't.
5. Do you make a meal at the library?   Yes, I do.   No, I don't.
6. Do you eat a few cookies at the movie theater?   Yes, I do.   No, I don't.
7. Do you use a computer at the library?   Yes, I do.   No, I don't.
8. Do you ride a bus to go to the movie theater?   Yes, I do.   No, I don't.
9. Do you write an address on a letter at the post office?   Yes, I do.   No, I don't.
10. Do you buy chicken at the library?   Yes, I do.   No, I don't.

Write about your neighborhood.

What does your neighborhood look like? Where are the library and grocery store?
Write four sentences. In each sentence use one group of the words below:
to the right of, to the left of, next to, across from

____

____

____

____

Word Log

Write the words you learned.

Shopping Words

m __ __ l

b __ __ __

c __ __ __

w __ __ __

n __ __ __

Money Words

d __ __ __ __ __

f __ __ __   d __ __ __ __ __ __

t __ __   d __ __ __ __ __

t __ __ __   d __ __ __ __ __

Coin Words

c __ __ __

ch __ __ __ __

p __ __ __ __

n __ __ __ __ __

d __ __ __ __

q __ __ __ __ __ __

Opposite Words

n __ __ __   o __ __

c __ __ __ __   e __ __ __ __ __ __ __

m __ __ __ __   l __ __ __ __ __